Jr. Graphic Mysteries

THE LOCH NESS MONSTER

Scotland's Mystery Beast

Jack DeMolay

PowerKiDS
press.

New York

Published in 2007 by The Rosen Publishing Group, Inc.
29 East 21st Street, New York, NY 10010

First Edition

Editor: Jennifer Way
Book Design: Ginny Chu
Illustrations: Q2A

Library of Congress Cataloging-in-Publication Data

DeMolay, Jack.
   The Loch Ness monster : Scotland's mystery beast / by Jack DeMolay.— 1st ed.
      p. cm. — (Jr. graphic mysteries)
   Includes index.
   ISBN (10) 1-4042-3406-3 — (13) 978-1-4042-3406-2 (library binding) — ISBN
(10) 1-4042-2159-X — (13) 978-1-4042-2159-8 (pbk)
   1. Loch Ness monster—Juvenile literature. I. Title. II. Series.
   QL89.2.L6D48 2007
   001.944—dc22
                                              2005037336

Manufactured in the United States of America

Contents

THE LOCH NESS MONSTER: SCOTLAND'S MYSTERY BEAST

WELCOME TO *LOCH NESS*, SCOTLAND!

THE LAKE, *LEGEND* HAS IT, IS HOME TO A STRANGE BEAST CALLED THE LOCH NESS MONSTER.

MANY PEOPLE BELIEVE THIS "MONSTER" IS ACTUALLY QUITE PEACEFUL.

SOME PEOPLE BELIEVE THAT THIS MYSTERIOUS CREATURE LOOKS LIKE AN **ANCIENT REPTILE** CALLED A PLESIOSAUR.

THE **EVIDENCE IS** SURPRISING!

THE LOCH NESS MONSTER LIVES IN LOCH NESS. IT IS A LONG, DEEP LAKE NEAR THE TOWN OF INVERNESS, SCOTLAND.

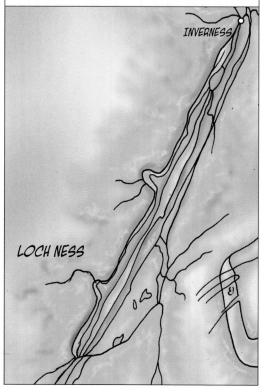

INVERNESS

LOCH NESS

OF ALL SCOTLAND'S LAKES, LOCH NESS IS THE MOST FAMOUS.

THIS IS BECAUSE THE LOCH NESS MONSTER, OR NESSIE, HAS MADE THE LOCH FAMOUS.

HINTS ABOUT NESSIE'S LIFE REACH FAR BACK INTO THE PAST.

THE EARLIEST HINT IS AN ANCIENT STONE **CARVING** OF A STRANGE SEA CREATURE.

IS THIS STONE CARVING **PROOF** OF NESSIE'S EXISTENCE?

WAS IT SIMPLY ARTWORK BY SCOTLAND'S ANCIENT PEOPLE?

THE FIRST SIGHTING OF NESSIE WAS IN THE SIXTH CENTURY.

AN IRISH **MONK** NAMED COLUMBA HEARD A STRANGE NOISE COMING FROM THE LOCH.

WHAT IS THAT I HEAR?

A MAN WAS BEING ATTACKED BY A STRANGE CREATURE.

ACCORDING TO HIS **BIOGRAPHY**, COLUMBA WAS UNABLE TO SAVE THE MAN.

NO! I AM TOO LATE!

COME HERE. I WON'T HARM YOU.

THE LEGEND SAYS THAT BECAUSE COLUMBA SHOWED NESSIE KINDNESS SHE NEVER KILLED AGAIN.

IN THE YEARS TO COME, THE LOCH NESS MONSTER MADE SCATTERED APPEARANCES ON LAND!

WHAT IS THAT? A MONSTER?

IN 1527, DUNCAN CAMPBELL SPOTTED NESSIE.

IN 1880, E. H. BRIGHT SAW WHAT HE SAID WAS A "TERRIBLE MONSTER."

IN 1912, WILLIAM MACGRUDER SAID HE SAW A YELLOW "CAMEL-LIKE" ANIMAL.

THE LOCH NESS MONSTER DID NOT MAKE NEWS AGAIN UNTIL AUGUST 1930.

THE THREE FISHERMEN SILENTLY WATCHED AS THE BEAST PASSED THEIR BOAT.

WHAT ON EARTH IS THAT?

LOOK OUT! IT'S RIGHT IN FRONT OF US!

THAT WASN'T ANY FISH! THAT WAS A MONSTER!

THEY WERE SURE THAT THE BEAST WAS THE LEGENDARY NESSIE.

THE FISHERMEN'S STORY SPREAD. SOON THE LOCAL NEWSPAPER RECEIVED REPORTS FROM OTHERS WHO CLAIMED TO HAVE SEEN THE MONSTER.

HUGH GRAY SAID HE SAW NESSIE IN 1933.

THAT THING WAS 40 FEET (12 M) LONG!

ROBERT KENNETH WILSON CLAIMED TO SEE THE MONSTER THE FOLLOWING YEAR.

I THINK I GOT A PICTURE OF IT DIVING UNDER THE WATER!

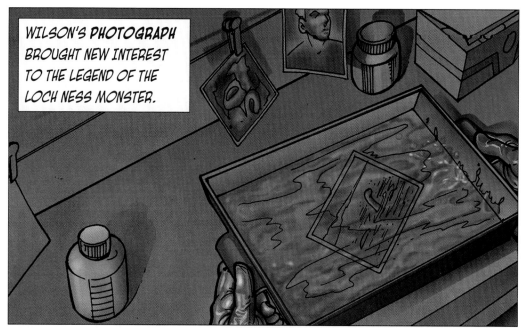

WILSON'S **PHOTOGRAPH** BROUGHT NEW INTEREST TO THE LEGEND OF THE LOCH NESS MONSTER.

WILSON SOON BECAME FAMOUS FOR HIS PHOTOGRAPH.

YEARS LATER SOME PEOPLE CLAIMED THAT WILSON'S PHOTOGRAPH HAD BEEN A **PRANK**.

HOWEVER, MANY PEOPLE STILL WANTED TO TRY TO SEE NESSIE FOR THEMSELVES.

PEOPLE FLOCKED TO LOCH NESS TO CATCH SIGHT OF THE LEGENDARY BEAST.

THERE IT IS! DO YOU SEE IT?

SURE LOOKS LIKE HER!

THROUGH THE YEARS, SCIENTISTS HAVE **INVESTIGATED** THE NESSIE LEGEND.

PERHAPS IT'S A PLESIOSAUR?

DO YOU REALLY THINK SO? HAVEN'T THEY BEEN WIPED OUT FOR YEARS?

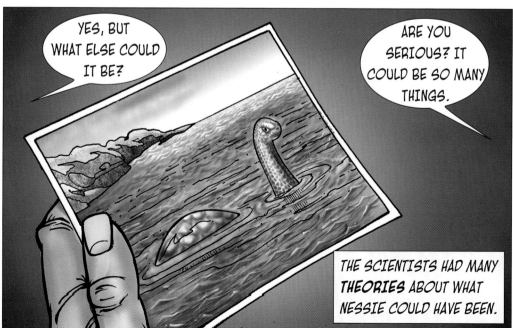

YES, BUT WHAT ELSE COULD IT BE?

ARE YOU SERIOUS? IT COULD BE SO MANY THINGS.

THE SCIENTISTS HAD MANY **THEORIES** ABOUT WHAT NESSIE COULD HAVE BEEN.

IT COULD HAVE BEEN AN ANCIENT CREATURE KNOWN AS A ZEUGLODON.

IT COULD HAVE BEEN A SEAL.

IT ALSO COULD HAVE BEEN A GIANT EEL.

PERHAPS IT EVEN COULD HAVE BEEN A WALRUS.

THERE WAS ALSO THE IDEA THAT NESSIE WAS NOTHING MORE THAN A FLOATING PLANT.

NESSIE ALSO COULD HAVE BEEN A GIANT **MOLLUSK**.

SOME PEOPLE THOUGHT NESSIE COULD HAVE BEEN AN OTTER.

OTHERS BELIEVED NESSIE TO BE DIVING BIRDS.

EVEN WITH ALL OF THESE THEORIES, SCIENTISTS CAME NO CLOSER TO UNCOVERING THE TRUTH ABOUT NESSIE.

THROUGH THE YEARS DIFFERENT SCIENTIFIC STUDIES HAVE BEEN DONE AT LOCH NESS.

THESE STUDIES HAVE INCLUDED THE USE OF HIGH-TECH TOOLS AND **SUBMARINES**.

SCIENTISTS HAVE ALSO USED CAMERA STATIONS AND UNDERWATER LISTENING TOOLS.

SOMETIMES EVEN HOT-AIR BALLOONS WERE USED TO LOOK FOR SIGNS OF NESSIE.

ALL THESE TOOLS WOULD HAVE HAD A HARD TIME SEARCHING LOCH NESS'S UNDERWATER CAVES.

THESE CAVES MIGHT HAVE PROVIDED MANY HIDING PLACES FOR NESSIE.

OVER THE YEARS THERE HAVE BEEN MANY SCIENTIFIC STUDIES.

HOWEVER, NO PROOF THAT NESSIE EXISTS HAS BEEN FOUND.

THE BBC TELEVISION COMPANY HAS STATED THAT NESSIE DOES NOT EXIST.

TO PROVE THIS CLAIM, THEY ONCE COVERED THE ENTIRE LAKE AREA WITH MORE THAN 600 SOUND SENSORS.

NO TRACE OF NESSIE WAS FOUND.

EVEN THOUGH MOST SCIENTISTS BELIEVE IT IS UNLIKELY THAT NESSIE EXISTS, THEY KEEP AN OPEN MIND AND CONTINUE LOOKING FOR PROOF.

UNTIL SOMEONE FINDS PROOF, PEOPLE WILL CONTINUE TO WONDER IF THE LOCH NESS MONSTER EXISTS.

THE END

Did You Know?

- As a result of Nessie's fame, Loch Ness gets a lot of visitors. Visitors spend around 40 million dollars each year at Loch Ness!

- Loch Ness is the largest freshwater lake in the United Kingdom.

- The study of legendary animals has its own branch of science, called cryptozoology.

- Nessie is the best-known cryptozoological creature in the world.

- In 1962, a group called the Loch Ness Investigation Bureau was formed. Its main purpose is to collect research about the creature.

Glossary

ancient (AYN-shent) Very old, from a long time ago.

biography (by-AH-gruh-fee) The story of a person's life.

carving (KARV-ing) Something that has been cut into a shape.

evidence (EH-vuh-dunts) Facts that prove something.

investigated (in-VES-tuh-gayt-ed) Tried to learn the facts about something.

legend (LEH-jend) A story, passed down through the years, that cannot be proved.

loch (LOK) The Scottish word for a large lake.

mollusk (MAH-lusk) An animal without a backbone and with a soft body and, often, a shell.

monk (MUNK) A man who has made certain promises based on his beliefs and who lives in a special house.

photographs (FOH-tuh-grafs) Pictures taken with a camera.

prank (PRANK) A trick that is played on someone.

proof (PROOF) Facts that show something to be true.

reptile (REP-tyl) A cold-blooded animal with lungs and scales.

sensors (SEN-sorz) Tools that pick up facts.

submarines (SUB-muh-reenz) Ships that are built to travel underwater.

theories (THEE-uh-reez) Ideas that try to explain something.

Index

B
Bright, E. H., 10

C
Campbell, Duncan, 10
Columba, 8–9

E
evidence, 5

F
fishermen, 11–12

G
Gray, Hugh, 12

I
Inverness, Scotland, 6

M
MacGruder, William, 10

P
plesiosaur, 15
plieosaur, 5
prank, 13

S
scientists, 15, 17–18, 20
sensors, 20
stone carving, 7
submarines, 18

T
theories, 15, 17

W
Wilson, Robert Kenneth, 12–13

Web Sites

Due to the changing nature of Internet links, the Rosen Publishing Group, Inc., has developed an online list of Web sites related to the subject of this book. This site is updated regularly. Please use this link to access the list:
www.powerkidslinks.com/jgm/lochness/